The SUBTLE ART of SURRENDER

A Practical Guide for the Recovery from
Anxiety, Depersonalization, and Derealization

JERZY ROGINSKI JR.

Archway Publishing books may be ordered through booksellers or by contacting:

Archway Publishing
1663 Liberty Drive
Bloomington, IN 47403
www.archwaypublishing.com
1 (888) 242-5904

Interior Image Credit: Jerzy Roginski Jr

ISBN: 978-1-4808-9499-0 (sc)
ISBN: 978-1-4808-9500-3 (hc)
ISBN: 978-1-4808-9501-0 (e)

Library of Congress Control Number: 2020916199

Print information available on the last page.

Archway Publishing rev. date: 01/21/2021

Background

I am a fully recovered former sufferer of anxiety, OCD, depression, phobias, panic attacks and depersonalization. I suffered for over 8 years, but found my way to recovery—and so can you. I remember what it was like to live every day feeling like I was going to die, that there was no end, and that suicide was the only option. I understand the feelings of panic, unreality, fatigue, numbness, obsession and more. I remember lying in bed all day filled with a rising tide of panic and anxiety 24/7, not wanting to leave my house, spending all my days researching and hoping to find some magical cure to my problem. I remember what it was like to go through benzo withdrawals. I remember trying all of the SSRIs, SNRIs and so many more, only to find myself getting worse. If this sounds like you, and if you're sick and tired of feeling this way and want to utilize a program that actually works, this book is for you. You will be working with someone who didn't just read about anxiety in college, or someone who sympathizes with how you feel, but has never felt the way you do; instead, I am someone who has lived it, studied it for years, day in and day out, and conducted thousands of hours of research, certification education, and much more.

In this book, I share my own story and the tools you need to recover. It is my highest hope that the rawness and truth of this book will help the millions of sufferers around the world feel less alone and find a true path to permanent recovery. You don't need any more wasted time, tears, and money on therapies and people who don't really understand what you're going through. If you're ready to recover, fully and permanently, then you've come to the right place

Are you tired of going to therapists, holistic practitioners, and doctors who really can't relate to you and don't understand the horror you are feeling? Are you tired of trying every single therapy known to man just to feel better for a little while, but then find yourself back to square one? Are you tired of going from med to med, supplement to supplement to find yourself feeling worse, defeated and hopeless? If you answered yes to any of these, then this book is what you need.

As a former sufferer of chronic fatigue, OCD, panic, anxiety, GAD, depression and depersonalization for over 8 years this book was written to give anyone in the same position the tools needed to fully recover from this condition. Using the science of neuroplasticity, a combination of psychology therapies such as; CBT, ACT, and NLP, Nutrition and Functional Medicine, Jerzy Roginski Jr was able to fully and permanently heal himself of these ailments.

NOTE 1:

To start off, I wrote this book as a guide to help those who are suffering with all forms of anxiety. This also means everything that comes with it, such as panic, fear, DP/DR, OCD, insomnia, brain fog, fatigue, depressed feelings, GAD and more. Considering how difficult it was for me to concentrate and initially absorb all this information, I wanted to make this book quick and to the point, delivering the essential information to you in a straightforward way, avoiding the storytelling that most books distract you with. I am extremely aware of how difficult the very act of reading can sometimes be for someone with DP/Anxiety—especially when reading about the condition. In fact, reading and hearing about your condition can often set off all sorts of negative thoughts. I've been there!

NOTE 2:

I am also writing specifically about my experience with and research of depersonalization, but don't worry if you feel that you are experiencing different symptoms and/or derealization. It's not a separate condition. I can tell you with 100% confidence from all the information that I've encountered in my 8 years of research that depersonalization and derealization are one and the same, they go hand in hand. It is my highest hope that this book will clarify any unanswered questions and give you the correct program and guidance to set you up for a full recovery.

NOTE 3: The fact that you developed anxiety and depersonalization is not your fault. You are not actually sick, and you are not actually ill. There is nothing really wrong with you. Although it may feel like you are sick, DP/DR is your body's natural reaction to trauma and anxiety. It is merely a symptom of anxiety and trauma, not some separate disorder. It doesn't matter how it came about. Even if your DP was caused by drug use, it's not your fault. You haven't "broken" your brain or done any permanent damage. In fact, you haven't actually done any damage. It's just a temporary natural reaction caused by stress. That's all. The fact that you have DP/DR is a great thing, because it means that you are ready to fully recover, and believe me… you can!

Disclaimer: Please note that the medical information contained within this ebook / document (and other documents contained in the Anxiety Recovery Guide) is not intended as a substitute for consultation with a professional physician and is not a recommendation of specific therapies.

Contents

This book is dedicated to my loving and supporting friends my family who always believed in me and helped me during the roughest times of my life. This book is also for all of those out there who are suffering and see no way out. No matter how many years you've suffered, or how bad you think your condition is, full recovery is always possible. Recovery is available to everyone, not just a select few.

God Bless,
Jerzy Roginski Jr

1

CHAPTER

What is Anxiety and Depersonalization?

Anxiety

Ah, good old anxiety, how are you, my old friend? Anxiety is a growing issue worldwide and affects millions of people around the world. We see countless sufferers going from doctor to doctor, pill to pill, and forum to forum discussing their anxiety and hoping to find a magic cure for their "problem". This cycle of searching and hoping continues the anxiety cycle around the world as sufferers help each other stay in the cycle, trapped by a flawed system that so often feeds on the helpless. Nothing seems to work in terms of traditional therapies such as CBT, SSRIs, anti-depressants, talk-therapy, herbs, detox, and magic diets. I know that sufferers are willing to try anything to feel better, only to find that everything we've tried thus far yielded little to no results, leaving us hopeless and defeated. If any results were achieved, they were short-lived, and left us back at square one, blaming ourselves for having these feelings. We find ourselves feeling utterly defeated, as though we have failed ourselves and the ones we love. We feel ready to give up at the slightest suggestion, fold the cards and call it quits on life. *Why me? Why is this happening to me? What have I done wrong to deserve this? I'm a good person, so why do I feel this way?* These questions and this story are so common among sufferers out there. You're not alone.

There's a big difference between just being afraid versus the typical nervousness that people get before an exam. A lot of people in society tend to brush off the severity of what "anxiety" actually is, which upset me a lot during my recovery. People who say they feel "anxious" before an exam or interview typically are just feeling nervous. Many people claim to have anxiety because they're worrying about the next paycheck or about their children, but these are normal human concerns. Anxiety, on the other hand, is fear and tension that is blown out of proportion to intense levels with no apparent cause. Anxiety is a severely heightened state of chronic fear and tension. It is not just your average worries of "how am I going to pay the bills." Instead, it is a nagging, annoying bug that seems to stick around no matter what we do. It's like walking with a knife in your back all day long and carrying the weight of the world on your shoulders at the same time. Only those of us that have felt it and experienced it can understand what it truly means. It is an impending feeling that something bad is going to happen. To have an anxiety disorder, or what I like to call an anxiety "state" or "condition", means that one is living in a constant state of worry and apprehension, waiting for and dreading what might happen next. Anxiety in all its shapes and forms basically sucks, but rest assured that this book will provide you with the tools you need to recover. Finally, you will have the truth at last.

Depersonalization/Derealization

Depersonalization usually comes after a prolonged period of anxiety or after a panic attack. This is described as a feeling of unreality, as though you have lost all of your emotions. It's a feeling of not really being there. It is as if you are watching yourself from the outside with a completely blank mind. It's like living in a constant fog, unable to remember your past or think in a clear manner. For me, this was one of the most difficult symptoms to deal with, but I got past it. I will describe this in greater detail later in the book. Most people that experience this sensation make the mistake of thinking that this is a mental illness, as their whole sense of self is suddenly gone and they feel dead on the inside.

The Reality of the Situation

The reality of it is that anxiety, DP, and DR are not actually mental illnesses. You are not sick, and there is no magic pill or anything outside of you that will fix it. There is no damage done to your body or brain, and there is no chemical imbalance causing you to feel this way. Nothing in you is actually broken; the real you is still there, just hidden beneath a protective shield of anxiety and depersonalization. Every anxiety sufferer has the same patterns, the same symptoms that show up in different ways, and the same road to recovery. What has happened is that you have created a fearful habit of thinking and self-centered focus that perpetuates a cycle of continued states of anxiety. Anxiety is a learned behavior; it's not an illness, but it's actually something your brain is doing to help you. It's only because of your habit of worrying and checking in on symptoms that they continue to exist.

Anxiety is just a memory of the past

Anxiety is a buildup of stress and past trauma that has not been dealt with or released. Trauma is stored in the body as a memory and DP is the protection mechanism in place to protect you from any future event that is similar to what you've experienced in the past. Thus, anything showing up in your life now that is remotely similar to that memory will trigger fear. When the body and mind is consistently triggered again and again it loses its resilience. The nervous system becomes more fragile and sensitized until fear and anxiety become your natural state of being. The fact that this state is based on a stored memory and learned behavior is great news! Since anxiety is the repetition of a stored memory of past trauma being played again unconsciously in the present, this means that we have the power to overwrite that memory, and I will teach you how to do that in this book. A good example of a real-life situation that describes anxiety is as follows. Everyone knows that when they touch a hot stove, it hurts and causes damage, but to *know* this, one must learn through experience. Therefore, when a person touches a stove and gets burned, the mind catalogues this: "Watch out, don't touch that again because it hurts." It learns to avoid the stove when it is turned on because it can physically harm the body.

Well, what does this have to do with anxiety disorder?

Anxiety disorder is something that is learned, just like the stove example; it is a pattern that develops in a similar way for everyone. It is a learned pattern of fearful avoidance that keeps the disorder alive. Allow me to explain...

How it develops:

A person can develop an anxiety disorder out of nowhere, but it typically develops when someone is going through a great deal of stress, drug abuse, or trauma, which can cause a buildup, followed by a panic attack or a nervous breakdown. The panic attack itself is a traumatic experience, or at least, it was for me.

Step one:

We start to feel overwhelmed. The stress builds and we begin to experience intense anxiety or a panic attack. These sensations send us into a state of doom and shock, as we have never experienced something like this before! *What is this? Am I dying? Am I having a heart attack? Am I going crazy and losing my mind? Am I dead?* Boom! We're in the heart of a panic attack and nervous breakdown, our mind rushing from thought to thought, making us feel like we're about to die and pass out. Just like the hot stove, this hurts us and we become bewildered by this bizarre experience. We interpret these feelings and sensations as a threat to our lives and believe them to be true. Our mind unconsciously registers this experience as being likely to lead to death, so the sensations trigger our fight-or-flight response. Our minds now begin to learn that this experience and all of the sensations that accompany it are something to fear. These sensations scare us to death. As a result of this fear and the traumatic experience, we become sensitized. Our nervous system is now in a state of sensitization, which simply means a heightened state of nervous arousal. This state of sensitization is uncomfortable because it comes with all the feelings of anxiety and won't go away.

Step two:

Instead of accepting these feelings as temporary and letting them go, we make the mistake of becoming afraid of the sensations of anxiety and panic, so we teach ourselves that this experience, just like the burning stove, is something harmful that must be avoided at all costs to survive. We begin to live in constant fear of what might happen next, when the next panic attack will occur, when the anxious sensations will return. We do everything in our power to make sure that this never happens again, because it was so scary, and we could die if it happens again... *what if it happens again*???? Does this sound familiar? We become indecisive and our mind begin to race in circles because we are sensitized. We begin to watch out for anything close to these sensations coming back, so we begin to live in a future-oriented state of fear.

Step three:

We develop a constant need to be on guard and make sure these sensations do not come up again, because if they do, that means danger, which we want to avoid, right? We begin to feel anxious about becoming anxious. Since we are feeling sensitization from the original experience, these thoughts become more powerful, even overwhelming us, to the point that we develop obsessions. We live in a state of constant fear of what might happen next, trapped by "what if" thinking and worries about the future. We begin to take less and less interest in the outside world and become deeply focused on our own inner world. We become more deeply consumed with ourselves, our thoughts and our feelings. We begin to avoid people, places and things that we believe will make us more anxious. We develop a habit of avoidance, as we believe that avoiding these situations makes us feel calmer.

Step four:

Our world begins to grow smaller and smaller as we increasingly remove ourselves from situations that we believe are intensifying our symptoms. We begin to constantly think about ourselves and our own sensations. We become suggestible to other people because it's so hard to make up our own minds. We begin to compare ourselves to how we were in the past and to other people. We believe that something in our past must have caused this, so if we find this deep-rooted cause, then all of our problems will go away. We spend a fortune on therapy in hopes that it will cure us, only to find that we get reassured and then end up back at square one. We believe that there is some magical cure outside ourselves that will make all the feelings go away. We become confused and wonder why we can't be like normal people, asking what we did to deserve this. We become consistently plagued by the way we feel and the state we find ourselves in. We begin to search for cures and answers on forums, YouTube videos, books, going to doctors, naturopaths, medications, herbs, yoga, meditation and more. We make it our life mission to get rid of our anxiety. We spend all of our time focusing on ourselves and our feelings, constantly fearing them and trying to get rid of them. This habit develops more for days, months or even years. We hope to find a magic pill, that one diet, the secret therapy, the special word, that singular miraculous thing that will make it all go away, but we inevitably find ourselves in the vicious cycle. We develop a habit that is known as an anxiety disorder. We are now trapped in the cycle of anxiety.

Step five:

All of this constant struggle and fighting against ourselves, with the continued failure to rid ourselves of these feelings, begins to fatigue our bodies and minds. We develop a sense of depression, feeling as though we have the flu all the time, which makes us even more afraid and unable to cope with ourselves. We continue to breakdown on a frequent basis, as we continue to worry about ourselves and our sensations. We lose our sense of confidence and the ability to make decisions seems like an impossible task. We become suggestible to other people and lose our inner voice and opinions; we start to please other people at our own expense. All of this continues to drain us until we become depressed, hopeless and even suicidal. The tension becomes too much to bear. We can't imagine taking another second of this living hell and then bam, we disconnect from our body.

Step six

Depersonalization and derealization set in because we have been disregarding the outside world and focusing on ourselves 24/7. Quite simply, our mind became so tired and fatigued that it couldn't take the onslaught anymore! It decided to check out and take a break. We mistake this feeling of unreality as a mental illness and think we're dead. Constant or fleeting feelings of DP/DR plague our day and now we're stuck with a full-blown anxiety disorder with depersonalization symptoms. Uh oh…. What now? Do you see how this pattern unfolds and creates the disorder? Does any of this seem familiar to you?

Note:

❖ DP/DR can also come on suddenly from a bad drug experience. Many sufferers I have spoken with, and sufferers who talk about DP/DR on forums explained that the condition came from a marijuana- or drug-induced panic attack. For some people, DP happens immediately after a traumatic experience, but regardless of how it comes about, the way out is always the same. Some people will find, like I did, that benzodiazepine withdrawal caused their ongoing anxiety disorder. If this feels true to you, don't worry... you can heal yourself from this! For information on how to micro-taper off of benzodiazepines, you can go to benzobuddies.org.

2

My Story

-In this chapter, I will share my life story as briefly as possible in the hope that something in my story will be relatable to readers. I want to illustrate my experience in an honest, uncensored way, to demonstrate that you are indeed not alone. Helping others really means a lot to me, and if reading this helps even one person in the world, all of my effort has been worthwhile.

My roots

I come from a Polish background, but I was born in Chicago. I come from a family that had to face a lot of trauma. My great-grandfather was murdered in Auschwitz during WWII because he always stood up for the right thing—for freedom and unity, just like I always have. I remember my grandmother telling me that the soldiers that fought by his side witnessed him being burned alive after he had attempted to throw himself onto a German tank with a grenade that had failed to discharge. She found out long after from the surviving soldiers what had happened to her father. My other great-grandfather was killed in front of his children and wife by the Nazis. After World War II Soviet dominance and communist rule took over Poland. I remember my mother telling me how much my grandparents had to struggle to make a living under the communist regime. My parents didn't want this life for themselves, of course, so they decided to leave their home country and immigrate to the United States. They escaped the communist regime in the hopes of finding a better life for themselves and their future family.

Family life

When I was just a child, I remember living in an apartment with a shared mattress and no furniture because we couldn't afford any. There were many days when my mother struggled to find enough food for us when we were growing up. My dad worked in a factory for 17 hours, 7 days a week, and my mom worked various jobs while trying to take care of us at the same time. She would go from jobs as a bartender to cutting hair to daycare. It was hard to find any decent job as an immigrant, so my parents took anything they could find. It was never easy for us growing up. Looking back, I recall as a young kid that we had a jar filled with coins. It was sort of like our family piggy bank. When we didn't have any money left, my parents would have to decide whether to buy food or gas with the coins, and they always seemed to choose putting money in the gas tank. Having gas in the tank meant that they could go to work and make more money to hopefully move out of the ghetto someday. Thinking about where we came from just blows me away. It was really tough living in an unsafe and impoverished neighborhood in Chicago. There were days when my parents would starve themselves to ensure that my brother and I were fed. I remember literally just eating bread with butter and sugar on it to get some sort of nutrition for the day.

Both of my parents left their families in the pursuit of happiness and had to wait 5 years before they were able to play the lottery to gain citizenship. My mother and father haven't seen their family during that entire process and it was hard to see them constantly struggle on their own. Day in and day out, I witnessed my parents choosing to struggle and make sure that my brother and I would have a better life. All they ever wanted was for us to have freedom and the choice to become something greater in our lives. I didn't know about all these struggles because I was so young. My mother and father told me the whole story when I was older because they felt I was ready. Young kids can't handle news like that, as it would put a lot of pressure on us. See, my parents are what I like to call "super protector" parents, perpetually present at every event to support us. My mom always dropped me off right in front of school and picked me up too; she went on every field trip as a chaperone and even volunteered in kindergarten just to make sure I was safe. Not living in the best area and going to a school where the kids were bullies and displayed violent and disruptive behavior made my mom afraid, so she did what she had to do to make us feel safe. In fact, she volunteered so much that our school offered her a job, which she accepted as a new source of income. Even though my mom and dad were always there for me, school was never easy. I never felt like I fit in at school, seemingly feeling much different than my peers. I was a rather shy and reserved kid, and was always highly intelligent in comparison to my classmates. I was also overweight and insecure, and would often eat to cover up my feelings of inadequacy. Throughout my school years, I was bullied daily and drew lots of attention as a mama's boy, since my mom was always around, in addition to my weight issues. I remember one particularly scarring event; I was at my locker when a classmate of mine pulled my pants down in front of everyone, leaving me standing there completely naked. I was horrified and embarrassed. I remember getting jumped in the gym bathrooms, being spit on, farted on, and kicked by a myriad of bullies. I can vividly recall kids keying my car and egging my family's house because I was weird and didn't fit in. I was bullied throughout grade school, middle school and even high school. This was incredibly rough on me, because my brother was totally different than me. He always had friends, hung out with the cool kids and took a very different path in life. His approach was to get involved with the older kids, to sneak out of the house, and pretend to be a badass, which is why he quickly got involved with the wrong people.

Brotherly Love

I was always jealous of my brother because he had what I had always wanted—coolness, to be liked, to feel good and wanted. He had a perfect six-pack body and could eat whatever he wanted. He had the confidence and the attention that I craved from other people. My brother saw this in me, but instead of trying to help me out, he used my weakness to his advantage. My brother, just like the kids at school, would bully me after I got home, calling me names and fighting with me. Basically, I had nowhere to go to feel safe. I was being bullied at school and then bullied when I got back home. This ate me up inside and made me feel chronically scared. It destroyed what little self-esteem I had, so I grew more closed off to the world, living inside my own shell instead. These experiences led me to not accept myself, which meant that I always tried to "people please" and be someone else. I thought that if I did what everyone asked of me, just the way they wanted, that I would finally be cool and accepted as one of them. My brother always had what I wanted, but he was so reckless that his behavior started to tear my family apart.

Don't judge a book by its cover

Moving along into my high school years, things started to go downhill pretty fast. At this point in our lives, my mom and dad both owned businesses and I began to work in my mother's company, helping her expand. We were fortunate enough to have moved out of extreme poverty into the middle class, and our family's success was only growing, or so it seemed. On the outside, all of our family friends and peers said how lucky we were, how great our lives were, with the biggest house on the block and the nicest cars, but what they didn't know was that deep down, my family was falling apart. My brother's behavior started taking a toll on the financial situation of my family, as well as the mental and physical health of myself and my parents. My brother got involved with bad people, which put he and I in trouble with the law several times. It tore my family apart emotionally to the point that all of us were losing sleep. I felt like I was in the middle of it all. I couldn't sleep and felt massive amounts of guilt because, on the one hand, I wanted to protect my younger brother and support him, but on the other hand, I wanted to be a good son and fair to my parents. I was living in constant fear of what terrible thing might happen every single day as a teenager. I went through many sleepless nights trying to figure out who I would stand behind—my brother or my parents. My parents always wanted us to do good, but he was misbehaving. There were many times that he got in trouble and I had to fight the urge to tell my parents that trouble was coming. Eventually, however, the trouble came out and my parents confronted me, arguing that I should have known better and should have told them. However, something inside me felt that it was my obligation to protect my brother; he was my younger brother and I was always afraid he was going to get hurt. To protect him, out of fear of what might happen, I would go with him everywhere, trying to convince him to change his mind and stop him from what he was doing. This landed me in a lot of trouble with my family and with the authorities, but I never gave up on my brother. It hurt me even more when we got in trouble, because we would then have to face my family. I would only hear, "Why didn't you tell us? You're older and should know better". No matter what choice, I made it was going to be the wrong one, because I would either be failing as a son or failing as a brother. It tore me apart. I remember one time where I had to hide the fact that there was a massive amount drugs being stored in our house from my parents just to protect my brother. Really, I had no choice but to keep this a secret, because even if I did say something my brother would blackmail me and I would lose my credibility with my family. It was extremely difficult to know that we had drugs in the house because not only did this threaten my brother, but also my family. I never asked any questions, and had no idea who the drugs belonged to. I just know that in that moment for some reason all I could think of was the movie *Dirty Dancing*. I kept thinking of what Patrick Swayze said: "There are people willing to stand up for other people, no matter what it costs them." Sure enough, I was one of them, and it certainly did cost me. I continued to take the hits and the falls, protecting my brother at all costs, no matter what that meant for me. My brother quickly learned that I would do anything for him, which he saw as a weakness and used against me. He knew I was scared for him and wanted to protect him, so he tried controlling me. He bullied me and made me feel small, just like the kids at school, meaning that I couldn't escape the bullying, no matter where I went. He would manipulate me into doing things I didn't want to be a part of, and we got into so much trouble as a result. At the time, my parents were working full time and trying to manage all our lives, while I sat there battling myself day and night, feeling like a fake, a liar and a cheater to the two people that had given up their lives for me. I could clearly see the chronic stress and frustration in my mother and father. My parents seemed to be aging quickly; they were always in a rush and constantly arguing. My family started to slowly fall apart as I stood there in the midst of it all. What shook me to the core during this time was when my mother became extremely ill. My father was already suffering from panic attacks, which he thought were heart attacks, and required frequent hospital visits. My mother was losing her hair from all the stress. One day, we were shopping at Walmart when my mother just passed out on the floor. We thought she was dead. She couldn't move and her body was so hot that we had no idea what had happened. I thought it was over, that she was gone for good. In that moment, I saw my whole life play out ahead of me without my mother. This brought me to my knees, as my mother had always been my best friend. I remember her being rushed to the hospital, having nothing to rely on but faith and hope that she was going to be okay. Thankfully, at the hospital, they were able to bring her back to us, but no one knew what had happened. The hospital simply sent my mom away and brushed it off as though everything was okay. Stress and problems continued to consume my family as the business grew. More success meant more stress, along with more court fees, additional legal issues and worsening health. For the next 3 years, my mother suffered chronic migraines, yet still got up every day to go to work. I watched her suffer in silence, torturing herself through every day to provide for our family. I watched her go from clinic to clinic and hospital to hospital, trying to figure out what was going on with her, but no one could figure it out. My mother told me that she lived in constant anxiety and depression, and that she thought about taking her own life, but she continued to work and live because of us, her children. All she had was a shred of faith and hope that things would get better. I lived every day in fear that she might be gone, that no one would ever fix her. I was also resentful about what was happening. I lived in anger and fear, becoming extremely ill and depressed myself. They finally determined that she had viral meningitis, which would continue coming back for life because of her weakened immune system, caused by the stress my brother and I brought into her life. I couldn't believe it, but our behavior was partially responsible for nearly killing my mother. I couldn't bear it anymore, and I fell into a deep depression during this time. I cried every day, holding knives in my hand, wanting to end it, as my life seemed hopeless. I couldn't help my mother, I couldn't help my brother, I had no friends, people disowned me and I had failed myself. Everything that was happening just made me crash. My need to have a perfect body, jumping from stimulant to stimulant, drug to drug, pill to pill, and diet to diet destroyed my physical and mental health. The pressure to be a manager in my mother's business and not ruin such a wonderful opportunity, all while going to school and studying, began to burn me out in a major way. I dragged myself through life like a zombie, feeling increasingly tired and depressed. Even though I felt this way, there was something inside that always told me to keep going, that this wasn't the end, that something big was waiting, giving me a light at the end of the tunnel. At the time, I didn't know what this meant, but I felt deep inside that something was indeed coming and that I was here to help others. I remembered what my grandmother told me: "Remember that you don't only live for yourself, but you live for others as well, and if you can save people from suffering or pain, do it. If you're able, just do it." I asked myself how the hell I was going to help anyone if I couldn't even help myself or my family. So, I fought hard and picked myself up. Many times I did it for myself, but most of the time I did it for my parents so they could be proud. To me, deep down inside I never felt like I could live up to the expectations I believed my parents had of me. This is why I continued to strive to be perfect, to be the best, and to never fail. It wasn't until my late twenties that my parents told me that they have always looked up to me and have been very proud of me. This really came like a shock to me, because I have always believed I was never good enough for them, and I always felt like I have failed them in some way. I wish I could have heard this sooner. It was because I held on to this belief that I was somehow inadequate that continued my downward spiral leading to many mental and behavioral issues throughout high school.

Psychiatrists & Pills

At this point in my life, I had to visit a psychiatrist because my high school teachers told my family that I was misbehaving, claiming that I couldn't sit still or pay attention. As a result, we did what any family would do, we went to see doctors and trusted what they had to say. The doctor told me that I had ADHD and that I needed to be medicated with Adderall. I was already fully depleted, fatigued and restless, and the doctors decided to prescribe me Adderall to cure my "ADHD". My family only wanted what was best for me and I don't blame them for anything; I didn't know any better either. All my parents wanted to do was get me help, even though they needed it more than I did. So, we went to multiple doctors to try and understand why I was feeling so unfocused, down and depressed. They only wanted the best for me, but those meds were the biggest mistake I could have ever made in my young life.

After being on these meds for a while, I could definitely focus, but I also couldn't sleep, I grew restless, I couldn't eat anything and I started to feel extremely depressed for no reason. I had no idea that these were common side effects of the medication. I believed that it was just me, and all in my head. At this point, things went south fast. I fell into a deep suicidal depression and began to abuse drugs. My friends and I would party every weekend, taking ecstasy and drinking until morning for days at a time. We would also smoke a lot of weed and dabbled with psychedelics, cocaine, and other pills. I never really enjoyed what we were doing at the time, and now that I look back, I realize that I was just trying to be cool and fit in. All I ever wanted was to be cool and be liked by people. After trying to keep up with this lifestyle for a while, I decided that I couldn't take it anymore and went back to the psychiatrist. They put me on so many meds that I had no idea what was going on. I was on Tegretol to stabilize my mood, Lexapro for major depression, and Seroquel to sleep. That was on top of the Adderall. They kept switching me from Lexapro to Paxil, to Effexor, to Effexor XR, to Prozac. Literally, I have probably been on every medication you can think of. They put me on Xanax, Klonopin, Ativan, Lorazepam and other benzodiazepines to help me sleep, since antidepressants are known to cause insomnia as a side effect. I literally lost my mind on these meds. The medications that were supposed to help me actually drove me crazy and launched me into what I felt was hell on earth. Being on these meds gave me suicidal thoughts, intense feelings of anxiety, and racing thoughts. Following that, I decided that I was done with medications and gave them up cold turkey. When I stopped taking my medication, I had my first panic attack and thought I was literally dying. It causes an utter feeling of despair, as if you are in the face of a lion, hearing and feeling every inch of his teeth biting into your skin. This is accompanied by a complete sense of confusion and a feeling of impending doom. It was an awful and traumatic experience. This nervous breakdown changed my life forever. After this first panic attack, I lived in a constant state of chronic tension, fatigue, and extreme panic. I had extreme levels of social anxiety and couldn't even leave my bedroom, developing agoraphobia. I laid in bed for hours trying to figure out what was happening to me. I couldn't understand my own mind and thought I was going crazy. I was deeply entrenched in the claws of benzodiazepine withdrawal, even though I had no idea this withdrawal existed. My doctors never told me that the medications they had prescribed would lead to withdrawals. Every one of them said that it was perfectly safe and that I would be fine to come off them, but they couldn't have been more wrong. I lived in a constant dream-like state of confusion; everything would be vibrating and spinning, as though I was drunk. I literally thought that I was having delusions or was a schizophrenic. I was about 21 at the time and had no idea what anxiety was, so I went back to the doctor. Of course, they put me on an SSRI antidepressant again, saying, "I think that you're struggling with depression, try this medication for a few weeks and come back for a follow-up." Again, I was stupid and naïve and just wanted help; I was so desperate that I would do anything to help myself feel better. After this visit, I filled my prescription and started the course of medication again. This medication not only didn't help my symptoms, but made everything worse. My mind constantly raced and I slept maybe 3 hours a night if I was lucky to sleep at all. I couldn't breathe and was in constant pain all over my body; every unexpected sound would scare the daylights out of me. I was so chronically fatigued from all the anxiety that I felt like I had a disease and the worst flu in the world that would never go away. I was so scared that I had lost all my friends because I wouldn't leave my house. I missed out on much of my young life because I was scared to leave my room. I couldn't be alone and I couldn't take care of myself. I stayed in bed for hours and days, just lying there, thinking and worrying and wondering what was happening to me. I remember getting up out of bed one day and saying, "If I'm going to suffer like this forever, then my life has no meaning." When my parents left for work, I grabbed a bottle of their whiskey poured myself a giant glass on ice, took my script for Prozac and Lorazepam and literally swallowed 90 pills of Prozac, 120 Lorazepam and some Adderall. This was my attempt at suicide. I made a Facebook post with all of my goodbyes to the world, stating that I would see everyone again in a better place, and that I can finally be at peace. Thank god that my friend Hunter saw this and rushed to my house, only to find me on my bedroom floor. My friend quickly called my parents and told them what had happened. I was rushed to the emergency room, but can't recall much of what happened on my way there. After detoxing from the initial overdose, I would find myself regaining consciousness by waking up to seizures and twitches in the hospital bed. Coming back from a suicide attempt was one of the most dreadful and insanely painful experiences I'd ever endured. I forgot what had happened and why I was there. For weeks, I had mini seizures, akathisia, restlessness, insomnia and hallucinations. I felt like bugs were crawling under my skin as my body continued to balance itself out from the overdose of medication. I literally had no idea who I was, where I was or what was going on. Nothing I did could make these feelings stop; I was totally helpless. When I finally came to my senses weeks later, I was upset that my attempt had failed, as I now had to continue to suffer. While all of this was happening, I discovered that I had also lost 2 close friends due to drug overdoses. The only thought that crossed my mind was, "Welcome to Hell." If the Bible described hell as a place of eternal torture, I felt that I was already there.

Hell on Earth

Over the next 7 years, I went through 3 near-death accidents, major surgeries on my gut and eyes, and extreme trauma to the body. Each accident and surgery added to my anxiety levels, which never went away after my initial experience. The accidents served to install trauma into my brain and further sensitize my already weak and fragile nervous system. Everything I ate made me sick and gave me foul symptoms; I couldn't even digest food, as it would get stuck in my bowels due to my constant state of extreme despair and tension. At one point I had to be hospitalized for an emergency surgery and almost lost my life. I had multiple bowel obstructions that started to shut my system down; they needed to operate immediately to remove it so that I could survive. Trauma after trauma continued to pile up on me and it seemed like I would never be able to catch a break or find relief. While going through all of this, I continued to work and go to school, which was a mistake. Can you imagine someone who can barely get out of bed still studying for a master's degree and somehow managing a well-recognized company in the state of Illinois? What the hell was I doing? I was completely lost. I had nowhere to go and frequently wanted to give up. I spent years going from neurologists to cardiologists, speaking to holistic doctors, trying different therapies, and testing every medication possible, but nothing helped. Imagine being in a position where not even the people you look to for help can actually help you. Not my family, friends or doctors. I was helpless. I spent all the money I earned on hospital bills, herbs, therapies and specialists. Thousands of dollars that I earned were lost, with no measurable improvement. I lost everything—my money, my health, my connection to people, my emotions... I lost myself. I experienced unreality, derealization, depersonalization and OCD like never before. I took connections, love, and emotions for granted because my ability to feel love or feel connected to anything was stripped away. I stood there totally lifeless and helpless. This continued for 7 years without a second of relief.

While I was sick with this condition, I studied everything I could about psychology, NLP, neuroplasticity, nutrition, and biohacking. I have read hundreds of books and thousands of articles on each of these subjects. I have talked with hundreds of people and experts in the field. I consumed every nugget of information that I could get my hands on. I became my own expert on the subject through experience and studying. While being sick over the course of 8 years, I obtained my Master's degree in nutrition, along with certifications in Functional Medicine, Coaching and NLP. I was obsessed with getting as much information as I could. I studied from morning until night working to figure it all out. And guess what?

I did.

Realization

At the age of 27, I finally began to apply everything I learned and my life began to change. After obsessively reading and learning for so long, I soon realized that this obsession with researching the condition actually fueled it, so I decided to give up the search and begin to apply all that I was learning. It was not until I gave up control and surrendered to the unknown that my life started to change. I began developing healthy habits and behaviors that would pave the way towards creating a totally new brain and body. I had to become a totally new me, while still living with the pain and suffering. I no longer chose to be the victim, but rather the hero of my own story. I learned that the only way out was to live my life as the person I wanted to be in the future. I had to literally fake it until I made it. This meant totally surrendering and accepting the horrible feelings, while also treating my body with respect and good food. This meant facing all of my fears in a state of total and utter surrender. I had to convince my subconscious mind that the traumas were over and that it was safe to be myself and relax. It was the greatest challenge I ever endured, because habits are so hard to break, especially since I had the habit of being sick and anxious every single day for almost 7 years! I was a master at being anxious, depressed and ill. I had become a victim—defeated, scared, and totally separated from the world. What I now had to do was become a master of being centered, healthy and authentic. By age 28, I was already almost there, but I felt that something was still missing to get me over that last hump. I just needed a little push to break out into total health, gratitude and well-being. That last hump was to find my purpose and meaning. I had to figure out how I would contribute to the world. I wanted to find a purpose and a reason behind all of this suffering and agony. So, I decided to spend the rest of my savings on NLP training, which completely transformed my life. I began to focus on my true passion and created well-being in my life. I rewired my old conditioning and became my best self. It wasn't easy to cure myself. In fact, it was one of the hardest things I could ever imagine going through in life. I wouldn't wish this process on my worst enemy. It was a bumpy road with more failure than I could have expected, but in the end, success was reached. I was finally cured and rebalanced. I finally decided to leave the real estate company behind and follow my heart, which was to change lives and inspire people to become their own hero through public speaking and coaching. That dream is what inspired me to write this book, start podcasts, create a new company, launch YouTube channels and act on my deep desire to give people the right information so they can avoid all those years of suffering I experienced. I want everyone to know that you are your own hero, and that nothing is impossible for you. If you really want something and are willing to do whatever it takes, you can make it happen for yourself, just like I did.

What I Learned

So, what are the lessons that I learned about life from this experience? Primarily, I learned that well-being comes first, and that the most important things in life are love, connection, freedom, peace and authenticity. I learned that no matter how hard life knocks you down, there is always a way. I learned to persevere and keep going, even though it felt like no one else truly understood me. I learned that it's never too late to follow your dreams and fulfill your purpose. I learned that whenever you're not aligned with your life path, something will tell you, whether you get sick, lose something or someone, or see things start going downhill. We must be grateful for the hard times and never regret any decisions. Remember that, you were only doing the best you could with what you had. If it were not for our hard decisions and difficult experiences, we wouldn't know what it is that we don't want. That's why the best way to know what we truly want is to learn from experience and identify what we don't want. That way, we can move toward becoming closer to who we really are. To become who we authentically are doesn't require changing or gaining anything; it is actually the opposite. We become who we really are by *unbecoming* everything that isn't us. I want everyone to remember one thing from this story: no matter how low you are in life, no matter what has happened to you, and no matter what your circumstances are, it's never too late to follow your dreams. It's never too late to change yourself. It's never too late to be the best you that you can be.

Symptoms of Anxiety and DP/DR

- I love each and every one of you deeply, and I know it may seem like an impossible task to you now, but trust me, the struggle is your biggest blessing and it will be worth it in the end when you fully recover!

J ust so that you understand how bad my anxiety was, I decided to create a list of all the symptoms I experienced so you don't think you're alone in your situation. Just because I don't list a particular symptom doesn't mean your condition is different. Everything you feel or think should be categorized as sensitized nerves and a tired mind. Don't let anything new scare you or trick you into thinking that it is something else. It's not. It's the same pattern playing over and over and over again.

Symptoms List

- ❖ *Negative outlook*
- ❖ *Lack of inner voice*
- ❖ *Lack of opinion*
- ❖ *People pleasing*
- ❖ *Not standing up for myself*
- ❖ *Self-obsession*
- ❖ *Spiritual realization*
- ❖ *Spiritual thoughts*
- ❖ *Thoughts about space and time*
- ❖ *Sudden feelings of oneness*
- ❖ *Sudden feelings of euphoria*
- ❖ *Restlessness*
- ❖ *Loss of identity and spirit*
- ❖ *Loss of self*
- ❖ *Out of body*
- ❖ *No thoughts/blank mind*
- ❖ *Constant tension*
- ❖ *Fibromyalgia*
- ❖ *Extreme fatigue*
- ❖ *Flu-like symptoms*
- ❖ *Drugs not working*
- ❖ *Loss of appetite*
- ❖ *Extreme sensitivity to noise*
- ❖ *Taking everything personally*
- ❖ *Inability to speak*
- ❖ *Irritability*
- ❖ *Stuttering and shaking*
- ❖ *Low confidence*
- ❖ *Floaters*

Hopelessness
Indifference
Inability to feel pleasure
Heart palpitations
Anger, Frustration
Questioning existence
Loss of smell, taste and touch
Inability to experience orgasm
Everything feeling unfamiliar
Feeling like I'm 90 years old
Depression
Inability to feel love or connection
Insomnia
Inability to feel emotion
Inability to cry
Nightmares
Waking up in panic attacks
Sleep paralysis
Extreme pain
Extreme fear
Digestive problems
Bowel obstructions
Sensitivity to criticism
Inability to relax
Mood swings
Avoiding confrontation
Agoraphobia
Hallucinations
Fogginess

❖ *Crawling bugs*   *Self-hatred*
❖ *Suicidal thoughts*   *Thoughts of harming others*
❖ *Violent thoughts*   *Loss of memory*
❖ *Loss of focus*   *Loss of libido*
❖ *Unreality*   *Object distortions*

CHAPTER

What I Tried

- Here I have included a list of all the herbs, medicines and therapies I tried, just so you don't think you missed anything for your recovery! None of these worked to cure me, by the way.

Things I tried

- ❖ *Spiritual retreats*
- ❖ *Water fasting*
- ❖ *noFAP*
- ❖ *Gerson therapy*
- ❖ *Isolation*
- ❖ *Adrenal fatigue diet*
- ❖ *Yoga*
- ❖ *Extended water fasting*
- ❖ *Leaky gut fix*
- ❖ *Ketogenic diet*
- ❖ *Meat only diet*
- ❖ *Functional medicine clinics*
- ❖ *Every doctor you can think of*

Alcoholics anonymous
Coffee Enemas
Chelation therapy
Juice detox
Resting
Antidepressants (all of them)
Meditation
Heavy metal detox
Candida diet fix
Vegan diet, Paleo diet
Sugar-free diet
Herbs
Guru workshops

- ❖ *Psychiatrist*   *Psychologists, Therapists*
- ❖ *CBT*   *EMF techniques, NLP*
- ❖ *EDMT therapy*   *Shock Therapy*
- ❖ *Spirituality*   *Self-help books*
- ❖ *Youtube Videos*   *Prayer*
- ❖ *Church*   *Hypnosis*
- ❖ *Getting a girlfriend*   *Sun-gazing*
- ❖ *Grounding barefoot walking*   *Quitting stimulants*
- ❖ *Hypnosis*   *Amino acid therapy*
- ❖ *5htp*   *St John's wort*
- ❖ *Valerian Root*   *L-Theanine*
- ❖ *Massages*   *Cold therapy*
- ❖ *Neurologist*   *Cardiologist*
- ❖ *Mayo clinic*   *Specialty disease clinic*
- ❖ *LSD*   *Xanax*
- ❖ *Mushrooms*   *Weed*

-The list of supplements I tried could go on forever. I tried every vitamin and supplement out there and it would take up too much space to give all the specifics. If it had anything to do with mood, brain fog, fatigue or anxiety, I spent my money on it and gave it a try.

Only a few of the supplements and techniques that I used from that list made a difference, but remember, none of these were a cure.

5-htp

Occasionally, to sleep, I would use 5-htp at 50mg. I would split the tablet in half and take it 30 minutes before bed. Sometimes it would help relax me and allow me to sleep, although I do recall it giving me some pretty wild dreams! 5-htp works by providing the building block for the body to create more serotonin. It is shown in studies that 5-htp is able to increase serotonin levels as high as some of the standard SSRI antidepressants, with fewer side effects. The cool thing about 5-htp is that it's readily available to cross the blood-brain barrier, which is like the doorway in your house, letting molecules in, and helping molecules get out. This means that it is easily accessible to the brain to make into serotonin, without having to go through the breakdown process of the amino acid L-Tryptophan. Try it out and see if it helps!

St. John's Wort (Perika)

I also did a trial with St. John's Wort, the Perika brand, for a few weeks and it helped me feel a little bit calmer, from what I can remember. I recall that it helped me quiet my mind a lot, which was great, but it didn't help with other symptoms. It is really up to the individual and how they respond to it. St. John's wort is believed to act just like an SSRI by inhibiting the reuptake of serotonin in the brain. It is also believed that this herb helps increase GABA levels in the brain, nature's calming neurotransmitter. I found that over the course of a few weeks, I did notice that I felt calmer in terms of my thoughts and mind, although it did make me feel sleepy at random times. All in all, it was a decent supplement and it helped with some symptoms, but not all of them. I know that it helped me quiet my thoughts when they were all over the place, which helped me move forward in my recovery. I eventually stopped taking since I felt that I didn't really need anything to recover. From my research and trials, I would highly recommend that you get the Perika brand and start slowly with one tablet and work your way up. Everyone is different, so experiment carefully and find the right dose for you.

KSM-66 Ashwagandha

Another supplement that was pretty effective was KSM-66 Ashwagandha. That one really made me feel nice and relaxed, with the feeling building up over time. I noticed that when I took 300mg of it, I immediately felt a lot calmer and level headed, which was a nice feeling. When taking it consistently, I noticed that I didn't overreact to situations like normal, and it provided an anti-stress effect and a somewhat apathetic attitude. Over time, though, I found that it diminished my motivation to do anything and made me feel like lying around all day, so be wary of this effect. Remember, everyone is different. I'm just sharing what worked for me from my experience. I still use this supplement and 5-htp when I want a really nice deep sleep or to wind down at the end of the week.

Multivitamins

I also used a multivitamin every single day—the Orange Triad from Amazon. I took 1 tablet two to three times a day to ensure that my body had all the essentials it needed to be healthy. The directions say to take 6 tablets per day, but less is more when it comes to any supplements, in my opinion. Plus, it is best to test for any deficiencies before saturating the body with high levels of vitamins.

Caution

Keep in mind that these herbs and pills are only supplements to your program of recovery. They are not a cure. Also, with 5-htp and St. John's Wort, be careful not to combine them, as they can cause a serious condition known as serotonin syndrome. Also, do not take these supplements if you're currently taking an antidepressant due to the potential for negative interactions. Please do your due diligence and take some time to research these supplements online, as there is plenty of information available to the public. For a specific supplement protocol, it would be best to get a hair mineral analysis, and a few tests with a functional medicine practitioner. If you have any questions or are confused in any way, you can always shoot me an email and ask me directly.

5

What I Thought I had

- Here I have included a list of all the illnesses I thought I had because of all the crazy symptoms I was experiencing. This is all I could think of, but I know there was a lot more.

Illnesses List:

- ❖ *Caffeine overdose*
- ❖ *Heart Disease*
- ❖ *Drug withdrawals*
- ❖ *Hypoglycemia*
- ❖ *Thyroid disorder*
- ❖ *Adrenal fatigue*
- ❖ *Cancer*
- ❖ *Brain fog*
- ❖ *Bacterial overgrowth*
- ❖ *Brain tumor*
- ❖ *Fibromyalgia*
- ❖ *Dopamine deficiency*
- ❖ *Vitamin deficiency*

Cardiac Arrest
Nicotine overdose
Sugar allergy
Diabetes
Chronic fatigue syndrome
Lupus
Candida overgrowth
Carbohydrate intolerance
Gut imbalance
Spiritual awakening
Serotonin deficiency
Gaba deficiency
Schizophrenia

- ❖ HPPD
- ❖ Post-acute drug withdrawal
- ❖ Borderline Personality
- ❖ Food allergy
- ❖ Copper toxicity
- ❖ Small bacterial overgrowth
- ❖ Dark night of the soul
- ❖ Anemia

Caffeine allergy
Insanity
Bipolar disorder
Heavy metal toxicity
Mercury toxicity
Brain damage
Alcoholism
Autoimmune disorder

6

Recovery Program

The Simplicity of Recovery

I created this recovery program from my years of experience and countless hours of research from various sources. The main points I am going to share with you might seem strange at first, but they're the only things you need to do to recover. All this time, you have been practicing being an anxious person by researching, fighting, avoiding and resisting. All of this fighting has gotten you nowhere and has kept you ill for months or years. To fully recover, you must do the total opposite of what you've been doing. You must rewire your brain and show your subconscious mind that it is safe to relax again. This means that you need to fully let go of the condition and to stop any anxious behaviors such as; constantly checking if your symptoms are still there, obsessively monitoring yourself, researching symptoms online, constantly going to doctors who tell you that it's just anxiety, etc. You have to try your best to stay away from anything that keeps anxiety at the center of your attention. I will explain this, and how it is done within the rules to recovery section.

Giving up the fight

You must fully give up the fight in terms of getting rid of your anxiety. Giving up is not a sign of weakness, but rather a form of acceptance. Giving up means that you no longer wish to fight with the anxiety anymore, you no longer wish to make it your priority, and you no longer want to fight with it or try to make it go away. All this time you have been trying to resist it, avoid it, make it go away or cure it, but it is this very effort and desperation that keeps you stuck in the cycle of stress. Your main goal should be to practice being a normal person again. This means living your life as if you had no anxiety, in total surrender to and acceptance of your feelings. This means doing everything you did before you had the condition, no matter how bad you feel. You must never let your feelings stop you from doing what you want to do. You need to continue going out with friends, going to work, and attending events, even if you don't feel like it. We are born in a natural state of acceptance, but when things begin to pile up, we develop stress and resistance to the present moment, which creates a disconnect from who we really are. This is why acceptance and wiring your mind back to the present is so crucial for your recovery. Acceptance is one of the tools used to rewire your mind and recover from anxiety. From my experience and the experience of many others, nothing else worked. I am sure if you picked up this book, you have already tried everything else. Nevertheless, I am by no means discounting other means of therapies and medications. If those worked for you then I am extremely happy for you and glad you found your way to recovery!

DP/Anxious Thoughts

Since anxiety/DP is just a habit of thought, all you have to do is change that habit. I know, this seems a lot easier said than done, but it can be done if you follow my steps. Thoughts are just thoughts; we have millions of them available to us, from the time we wake up to the time we go to sleep. When anxious, we tend to have negative thoughts and the only thing we need to do to deal with these thoughts is to nothing at all. Sure, these thoughts might be scary, weird or irrational, but they don't matter. To recover from this, all you need to do is accept these thoughts and focus your attention on what you're doing. You must let go of trying to figure yourself out. Stop trying to figure out each thought and the meaning behind it, as this is pointless. Stop trying to think certain thoughts and force yourself to think different ones, because that doesn't work. Simply let everything be as it is. In time, your mind will quiet down again.

The only reason you're having such a reaction to these thoughts is because you have anxiety and are sensitized—that's it! There is no harm done, no permanent damage, no real illness here. You must not judge every thought or follow every thought down the rabbit hole. The only way to get rid of the thoughts is to let them be. Don't focus on them or judge them, just allow the time to pass. In time, thoughts return to normal and calm down once you rewire your mind for acceptance. These thoughts are only coming up because you have been in a state of habitual resistance and worry, but they're not real. They are not who you truly are. Be an *observer* of your thoughts, instead of a constant moderator, and let them come and go as they please.

A few words on Meditation

Everywhere you look online, someone is selling the idea that meditation is great for anxiety! People claim that it will help remove feelings of depression and anxiety, even if you just meditate for 30 minutes a day! Wow, how great is that? Meditation is a great practice, and I'm not one to judge without trying something first, but I'm going to be honest with you... from my experience, and for many of my clients, and other recovered sufferers, meditation was counterproductive to their recovery. This does not mean it won't help you; try it out for yourself and see if it helps or not. If you find that meditation makes you feel more relaxed and grounded, then great, keep up the good work. I know I tried to meditate my thoughts and feelings away. I practiced meditation for 3 hours a day, and it did absolutely nothing but make me feel worse. It made me feel more dissociated and more anxious, and I felt that I could never relax. It made me feel like I was falling deeper and deeper into the hole. The problem is that, with an anxiety disorder and dissociation, we're already deeply concerned with how we feel. We are so inwardly focused and preoccupied with ourselves that meditation only creates a set amount of time to be more focused on how we're feeling and what we're thinking. As sufferers, we already habitually check in on our symptoms, and monitor ourselves closely, watching for them to go away. This is the total opposite of what we want to accomplish here. The goal is to get the focus off of ourselves and our sensations and focus our attention back onto life, and the outside world. This is why meditation can even worsen feelings of disconnection. What we want is to be able to feel again, to feel grounded and connected, while meditation will only serve to fuel the habit of introspection and checking in on how we feel. Unless it helps you feel more grounded, it is best to totally avoid this practice until full recovery is reached, and even then, I've seen many people experience depersonalization from meditating too long and too often.

Defining Resistance

So, what exactly is resistance? To further illustrate how resistance works against you in recovery, I want to explain it a bit more deeply. In an anxious or traumatized state, when we are presented with a certain feeling or a thought, we can resist it in many different ways. One way we can resist is by either trying to think our way out of our feelings or by analyzing our feelings and thoughts until we fall down a rabbit hole of negative thinking. We can also resist through fighting against our feelings, primarily by wishing them away or wishing that things were different. We can also resist our feelings by frantically distracting ourselves, which is essentially trying to run away from and avoid them. We can also resist our state by tensing up our body when we experience triggering thoughts and symptoms. We may also try to cover up our feelings with drugs, alcohol, herbs, pills and supplements, all of which are counterproductive to recovery. Using the above coping mechanisms, we create a habit of avoidance towards our current state. This habit builds up over time until it becomes unconscious. Just like tying your shoe, you do it enough times that you don't even have to think about it, you can simply do it. This unconscious response of avoidance perpetuates a state of urgency and tension in the body. It creates a habitual pattern of unconsciously reacting with fight-or-flight symptoms towards everything in your environment, even though no real threat is present. The subconscious mind believes that there is a threat and tries to protect you by constantly creating a fight-or-flight response in the body. The tension mounts and continues without you even being aware that you're the one doing it. How does it do this? Well, when you resist something in thought, you are unknowingly and unconsciously tensing up your muscles and body, which alerts your nerves and mind that there is something to either fight or run away from. This continued cycle constantly places stress on a body that is already stressed, never giving it a chance to repair itself. This is what leaves many of us exhausted, fatigued by flu-like symptoms, and deeply depressed. If you were to make a fist and squeeze it as tightly as possible for as long as you could, your arm would eventually fatigue due to lactic acid buildup, so you would be forced to let go of that tense and tight fist. You can try and try and try, but no matter how hard you try to hold that fist tight forever, you will always discover that you run out of gas and need to relax to replenish your energy stores. Now, imagine that this fist is your whole being, your whole body and existence. With continued resistance to your thoughts and feelings, you have created a habit of responding to your thoughts and feelings by creating tension in your body, just like in a fist. You unconsciously react all day long with varying levels of muscular tension, which is a form of resistance towards your current experience. It's like holding your fist tight, but the fist is your body, and it never lets go! This continued reaction of resistance leaves tension in the body. This tension builds and builds until you eventually have a panic attack or become so exhausted and fatigued that your mind checks out into a foggy, dream-like world. It's no wonder that we feel so exhausted, that our mind is foggy, that our world seems unreal, and that we feel weak and on edge. We literally use up all of our energy fighting ourselves, tensing ourselves up and spending ourselves daily. It is no surprise that we can't think clearly, or that our mind goes blank, or that we feel depressed. It's almost inevitable that we would feel this way. It's totally normal in such circumstances to feel the way we do, considering that each day our foot is flooring the gas pedal! Don't simply assume that something is wrong with you. Basically, your body is responding exactly in the way it is supposed to do given the conditions you're creating for it. The good news is that these conditions are totally reversible; however, it is up to you to do it! Our goal here is to reverse this process so that we replace the habit of resistance with the habit of acceptance. The rules I have created in the next section will show you exactly how to do this so that you can begin your recovery process.

Recovery Rules/Steps

- Here I have included a list of the exact way to recover. If you implement these steps, just like many others, you will be on your way to recovery. It takes about 2-3 months to desensitize the body, but all you need for recovery can be found in these steps.

How to rewire your brain

RULE 1:
Total Surrender And Acceptance

Even though these feelings can be overwhelming, you must learn that fighting them is showing your mind that something is wrong and that danger is present. You can fight your feelings by trying to think them away, drink them away, or by physically tensing against them. Doing so just leaves the fight or flight response activated and therefore continues the uncomfortable sensations. If you avoid the feelings, then you're also showing your mind that they are something to be afraid of and that there is danger present, so it isn't safe to relax yet. Surrendering and giving up is not a weakness. It means allowing your body's natural fight or flight processes. It means to stop making your feelings the center of your attention, and move on. The only way to show your mind that there is no danger present is to behave calmly. This means getting up in the morning, slowing your movements down, breathing slowly, and focusing on what you are doing, not on how you are feeling. Do everything you would normally do, even while feeling like utter garbage, do not resist it. Acceptance is not the same thing as putting up with the feelings and simply going about your day. No! Acceptance is about being there as a witness of the feelings, but not becoming them, not getting upset by them anymore, not wishing things were different, and not waiting for them to go away before you can start living. Giving up is about trusting that your mind and body is much smarter than you and that it knows how to bring itself into balance without your input! Trust me, your input, your trying, your fighting and needing to be cured is what has kept you sick this whole time. It is so simple, but so hard to do because you have practiced avoiding, fighting and resisting for so long! It's time to just step aside, and get out of your own way. This new habit of acceptance might take a long time to get down, but once you're in true acceptance, you can recover. So... how do you stop fighting your anxiety?

To clear up what true acceptance means, I typically explain acceptance as a mind and body integration. There are two components to acceptance if you want it to work properly; one must accept the thoughts and sensations, which is mental acceptance, as well as loosen the body, which is physical acceptance. Given our habit of resistance, we have unconsciously developed a pattern to try and fight our thoughts and feelings, or avoid them entirely. We naturally want to change our thoughts or run away from them, so we unconsciously tense our body towards the sensations and thoughts. However, we must reverse this process to heal our nervous system. To accept your thoughts and feelings means allowing the thoughts and feelings to be there without questioning them, without trying to figure them out, and without your input or fear of them. Also, while practicing this mental aspect of acceptance, we must create a state of calm in the body, which is achieved by allowing your body to be as loose and relaxed as possible, while simultaneously accepting the thoughts and feelings. This is what many spiritual teachers mean by "letting go". Just like the clenched fist example, you must let go of that tight hold you have on yourself in order for your body to recover and regain its vitality. To practice letting go of muscle tension, you can forcefully tense up your whole body as hard as you can, and then let go. Practice doing this until you get good at noticing what it feels like to be tense, and how you can let go of that tension. Doing this repeatedly will allow your body to recognize that you don't have to fight or flee the situation, and that you're actually okay. Making this your new habit creates a calm physiological state in the body that allows the release of stored trauma, anxiety and tension. This means being aware and vigilant throughout your day and noticing when you tense up your muscles; at that point, you should instantly release this tension and get back to what you were doing. Using muscular tension releasing, loosening the body, and allowing all your thoughts and feelings will begin the process of desensitization. You must be vigilant and do this all the time, until it becomes your new unconscious habit. Remember, just because you're releasing tension in the body consciously doesn't mean that your thoughts and symptoms will go away immediately. You may still feel discomfort for a time, but the goal here is to release the tension in the body as much as possible, to the best of your ability. When used in conjunction with total acceptance, this will begin the release of stored trauma and anxiety, leaving you free and in control once again.

RULE 2:
Stop Researching The Condition

Only anxious people anxiously research and jump from forum to forum, worrying and trying to figure out why they feel the way they do. If you want to recover, you must stop researching the condition. The goal is to rewire your brain and forget about this habit. While continuing to accept your thoughts and feelings, you must also focus your attention on something else. Find something you love to do and do it all the time to keep your mind busy 24/7. Never look up forums, videos or read other books on this endless subject! You have been doing this for God knows how long and it hasn't worked! You should stop this habit now and give up the search because there is no magic cure and there is no magic pill because there is no real illness present! You have a tired mind and body! Your nerves are sensitized, and that's it! The mind and body will heal itself as long as you get out of the way and let it! Researching the condition only serves to remind you that you should be feeling anxious, and we want to avoid that at all costs.

RULE 3:
Stop Complaining/Talking About Anxiety

You're not sick and you don't need to be complaining to other people about how you feel all the time. You must stop complaining and instead fill your mind with positive input. Complaining is a really bad habit and keeps you stuck in yourself and your problems. Plus, no one wants to be around someone who complains all the time anyways! Try to notice how often you complain and make the conversations about you, your problems, and your feelings! This is a negative habit, and this is not you... this is your *anxiety*. Anxiety makes you self-centered, even though you are probably a very selfless and caring person! Stop the complaining! Surround yourself with positive people and never bring up the topic of how you feel in a conversation. Doing this will only serve to remind you of your anxiety. It is so easy and natural to complain about how you feel and how sick you are because you get a sense of connection from that and you feel loved, but you do not need it anymore. You are strong and you can do this! Plus, you don't want people to constantly ask you how you're feeling and how your anxiety issue is being handled. You don't want people to treat you as if you are sick because you are actually perfectly healthy and readily available for anything. It is okay to sometimes vent to the ones that you love, but it's best to keep this to a minimum. I know sometimes it feels really good to just let it all out on someone who's there to listen, and that's totally okay. What is going to hinder you in this process is continuing to talk and complain about how you feel every day to the ones you love. Those that don't have anxiety disorder will have trouble understanding how to help you, which is why it's best to talk to people that have been through this condition, and those that are recovery-focused, not symptom-focused. Any conversation that talks about feelings, symptoms, fear and a poor-me attitude can limit growth throughout this process. If people ask you how you're feeling, you don't have to lie about how you're feeling, but you should actively diminish the 'importance' of the depersonalization and anxiety.

Regardless of how anxious or depersonalized you feel, you must live your life as normal. You want people to know that you're 100% available for everything and I mean everything no matter what!

If you have already been to many doctors and therapists and they say that all you have is anxiety, then you don't need to visit them anymore. This is an anxious habit that is counterproductive to your recovery. If you need any reassurance, just reach out to me and I'll do my best to help. Going to therapy is great, and telling them about this program is awesome, maybe you can work on it together. My advice is to make the focus of therapy on things that are going on in your life, and not about your anxiety. Remember we want to forget about our anxiety and get back into our life. Going to the therapist and complaining about your anxiety, symptoms, and feelings isn't going to get you anywhere. All you're doing is reminding yourself that something is wrong, that you are an anxious person; you are only reinforcing this pattern and belief system! This must end! Many therapists like to dig deep into your past and find out some sort of a subconscious cause for your anxiety. This endless search into the past about what caused your condition is the condition itself. Looking in the past removes you from the present. It does not matter what the cause was, recovery is possible for everyone.

RULE 4:
Create A Vision

What helped to keep me focused on a better and brighter future was creating an ideal vision for myself. In clear detail, I wrote out what I wanted in my life as a career, how to feel, my relationship and my ideal life! I wrote it out as though I already had it and continued to read it all the time, throughout the day, to keep myself focused on where I was going. This helped tremendously. For example, I wrote:

I am happy, content and grateful for what I have. I have a beautiful home next to the ocean. I am married to a beautiful brunette woman, with green eyes who shares a passion for fitness and helping others. I feel connected and peaceful and am influencing the world in a positive way.

When coaching clients, I help them create this vision, as well as implement a life wheel to determine what is off balance in their lives.

RULE 5:
Get Out And Live Again

Just get out there and start living your life again. Say yes to every invitation and go out to every event. This doesn't necessarily mean you will enjoy it or feel amazing while doing it, but who cares? Do it anyways. You might never feel like doing any of it, but you must. This is the only way to reintegrate yourself into real life and show your mind that everything is okay. It doesn't need to keep protecting you from the outside world, but you need to show your mind that!

When you get out and do things, you will, for a time, probably feel anxious and depersonalized. That doesn't matter. Any time you don't do something because of how you feel, you are reinforcing the habit of anxiety and fear. You're teaching yourself again that you must avoid things because of how you feel. We do not want that! Doing it, no matter how anxious or depersonalized it makes you feel, tells your brain that you can do anything. So, get up and do it! These small actions tell your brain that you're safe, and that you can do it again. This is absolutely necessary, as it tells your subconscious that you don't need to feel anxiety anymore. Whenever you start to think about anxiety or DP, do something else:

- ❖ Exercise
- ❖ Walk
- ❖ Yoga
- ❖ Read a book
- ❖ Watch a movie
- ❖ Play your favorite video game
- ❖ Youtube videos (NON-DP Related)
- ❖ Learn to juggle
- ❖ Learn a new language
- ❖ Learn a musical instrument
- ❖ Go to work
- ❖ Volunteer
- ❖ Read your vision
- ❖ Repeat your vision
- ❖ Etc…

It's always best to create some sort of a schedule so that you know exactly what you're going to be doing that day. Grab a calendar and literally fill it up with activities so you don't have any time to focus on DP and its symptoms. Creating an organized schedule removes decision-making fatigue and unnecessary anxiety because you now know what is coming in the future, since you're literally creating it with your schedule! How cool is that? If you stopped pursuing any hobbies that you used to enjoy because of your anxiety, now is the time to pick those back up and do them again! Whether it was painting, knitting, music, video games, anything! Don't let anxiety be an excuse for you not to enjoy yourself. Never structure your life around your anxiety, this will only show anxiety that it is in control, and we don't want that! Furthermore, you might be surprised to find that when you really dive deep into a hobby that you enjoy, you totally forget that you have DP in the first place! *This is what we want.*

RULE 6:
Create A Sleep/Wake Schedule

You cannot stay in bed all day! Set an alarm clock for the same time every morning and get up at that time, no matter what, no matter how much you slept or didn't sleep the night before... get up and do this! Also, do not go to bed unless you're actually tired. You don't want to be lying in bed ruminating about how you are feeling, so stay occupied until you actually feel tired. When I couldn't sleep, I would just read my vision all night long! When you wake up in the morning, don't stay in bed. Get up immediately. Don't sleep in. You don't have the flu or a cold, and you're not bedridden. When you wake up, get up. Put on some upbeat music and grab a glass of lemon water to kickstart your metabolism. Take a cold shower in the morning, as this will help your body wake up and shake off the fog from the night before! Exercise, read, and prepare breakfast. Get out into the world!

RULE 7:
Stop Looking For Solutions Everywhere

Stop the habit of looking for solutions everywhere. Doing this always keeps anxiety and DP in the forefront of your mind and you want to avoid doing this—no exceptions. Finding all of these quick-fix solutions from doctors / therapists / alternative therapists / forums / websites is part of the condition. Anxiously searching for solutions is your anxiety behavior. This is why you must stop this behavior at once! You will never find an instant cure from any of these. The only reason you should do this is to get temporary reassurance, but we both know that this never lasts long and leads you right back into the same cycle of researching and trying to find another cure, as if you had missed some critical little nugget of information. Trust me, there is no nugget of information that you need. Everything you need is in you and in this guide. Stop depending on other people to help you, trust yourself and your higher power, if you believe in one, that you can recover. You don't need anyone or anything outside of yourself! When you feel the urge to look up DP online, do something else instead. Get distracted. Do that *every time*.

RULE 8:
Repeat Your Vision And Affirmations

After creating an ideal vision for your life, create a short version that you can repeat to yourself all day while you're working and living your life as normally as possible. For example, my vision and the affirmation that I repeated in my mind was:

I am happy, I am relaxed, I am excited and fulfilled every day. Money, love, fun and gratitude flow to me and through me every day. I change lives for the better.

I thought about this all day long, like a broken record player. This is a great tool and technique I used to get the thoughts of DP out of my head, because we can only think about one thing at a time. TRY THIS OUT!

RULE 9:
Stop The Pity Party

Obviously, a regular person wouldn't be blaming themselves and hating themselves because they broke their leg and can't walk.

They wouldn't beat themselves up over it and continue to focus on the fact that they can't walk. Honestly, it's no one's fault that you have this condition and it's pointless to blame yourself. It will only keep you stuck in a negative cycle and prolong your *temporary* condition. Stop being the victim of your situation and blaming people, yourself, places and things. It's easy to play the victim, as it allows you to avoid taking responsibility for yourself. That way, other people can always be there to take care of you.... It's time to move on and take ownership of who you are. Your goal here is to not give any importance or attention to the condition. Give up, surrender, accept and move on!

RULE 10:
Exercise

Join a gym, establish a workout routine and go every day of the week, if possible. You can try swimming, tennis, sports, running or anything else that you think that you might enjoy.

It doesn't matter what you do, but you must exercise. It doesn't matter if you've never exercised before... you need to do it, as this is a crucial part of your recovery. Exercise will help expend all that restless and anxious energy that has been stuck in your body and will allow the process of recovery to unfold more smoothly for you. The way you exercise will be determined by the current state of your body. If you're in a state where you are extremely fatigued, intense exercise can be counterproductive, so start slow and small, but be consistent. There is no need to push yourself beyond your limits when you first start. Begin by taking a walk in the morning, go for a bike ride, or try doing some yoga. Try anything that is slow and soothing to start. Doing exercise outdoors is the most beneficial because you can get fresh air, connect with nature, and boost your vitamin D levels from the sun. Plus, being outside in the sun has been shown to increase serotonin levels, which play a key role in your mood. As your body begins to regain its strength and energy levels, slowly ramp up the intensity. With my clients, we always start off with a small set of goals and work our way up to build a stronger and healthier body. Based on a few functional medicine tests, we create a specific exercise program that benefits the individual. It all really depends on your current state of health and fitness, which is why all of these recommendations are somewhat non-specific. When in a state of chronic fatigue and exhaustion, it's best to avoid any crazy and intense exercise, as this just depletes the body's energy stores even more. In this phase, it is more important to focus on reviving the body through proper nutrition, supplementation and revitalizing exercise, such as yoga, tai chi and stretching.

Benefits of exercise:

1. *Exercise has been shown to improve your mood and decrease feelings of depression, anxiety and stress.*

2. *Exercise produces changes in the parts of the brain that regulate stress and anxiety. It can also increase brain sensitivity for the neurotransmitters serotonin and norepinephrine, which relieve feelings of depression.*

3. *Exercise has favorable effects on the pain associated with various conditions. It can also increase pain tolerance.*

4. *Gives you a tremendous sense of well-being.*

5. *Helps give you strength and lose weight.*

6. *Regular physical activity, regardless of whether it is aerobic or a combination of aerobic and resistance training, can help you sleep better and feel more energized during the day.*

7. *Engaging in regular physical activity can increase your energy levels. This is true even in people with persistent fatigue and those suffering from serious illnesses.*

8. *Daily physical activity is essential for maintaining a healthy weight and reducing the risk of chronic disease.*

9. *Moderate exercise can provide antioxidant protection and promote healthy blood flow, which can protect your skin and delay signs of aging.*

10. *Regular exercise improves blood flow to the brain and helps brain health and memory. Among older adults, it can help protect mental function.*

11. *Exercise can help improve sexual desire, function and performance in both men and women. It can also help decrease the risk of erectile dysfunction in men.*

RULE 11:
No Drugs

Illegal drugs are not an option during your recovery. They will only cause further imbalances in your body, which should be pretty OBVIOUS, but many people think that if they smoked weed and it gave them depersonalization, then maybe if they smoked weed again, it would somehow "snap" them out of it. This couldn't be further from the truth. I know this because I have tried it and many of my clients have made the same mistake. Making these mistakes just prolonged the recovery process for myself and many other sufferers. Any mind-altering drugs at this time will seriously interfere with your recovery. We want to stay in balance as much as possible. Most drugs will disrupt brain chemistry, leading to more mood problems in the long run. I know that I tried to self-medicate with various drugs, none of which worked in the long term. I know that for me, most of them just gave me adverse reactions due to my highly traumatized state.

RULE 12:
No Caffeine

This should be another pretty obvious one! Caffeine is a stimulant that increases the stress hormones in your body. It literally shoots adrenaline into you and activates your flight-or-fight response to give you perceived energy through this state of emergency. This is the opposite of what you want. Even though you may feel fatigued, you're not actually sleepy or tired. You will probably think like I did—that you are just tired and exhausted or somehow not fully awake. It may feel like this, but your mind is just in a protective dream state. Underneath the fogginess is a very clear head. Caffeine will only make you more anxious and deplete your energy even further, so stay away. Caffeine literally creates a state of urgency in your body. It activates your fight-or-flight response, whereas our goal is to create a sense of safety in the body. Caffeine increases cortisol and adrenaline in the body, which increases heart rate and muscular tension in the body. To recover fully, we don't want anything that is going to add tension, since we are doing that enough already with our thoughts and reactions. This will only add fuel to the fire and must be avoided. For more information on caffeine, a great book called *Caffeine Blues* really illustrates how it can mess up your mental health!

RULE 13:
No Nicotine

Nicotine is also a stimulant and can aggravate your symptoms by increasing your heart rate, making your hands tremble and increasing blood pressure. It is best to cut it out or at least try to cut down on nicotine usage over time. If you're a heavy smoker or vaper, cut down gradually to avoid withdrawal symptoms. Your goal is to remove anything outside of yourself that can be a stressor. Nicotine is a stressor, as it increases stress hormones in the body, which will only prolong your recovery. Remember that the body can only start to heal when it is not in a state of stress, and this is done through the techniques outlined in this book and by removing anything that artificially boosts stress hormones.

RULE 14:
No Sugar/ Alcohol

Sugar

When you suffer from anxiety attacks, you tend to become hypersensitive to your body. You fear your anxiety attacks, and you notice every single time that you feel tired, lightheaded, sick, etc. You notice each and every ache and pain, and you notice when you're not thinking clearly. Every time you notice any of these changes, your anxiety spikes.

Sugar itself doesn't necessarily cause any of these sensations, but sugar does stimulate various sensations in your body. Glucose— and the insulin released to counter glucose—can cause fatigue, difficulty thinking, blurry vision and general ill feelings. For those without anxiety, many of these symptoms go unnoticed. However, for those with anxiety, each and every one makes you worry that a panic attack is coming, and that fear increases your likelihood of getting one. Furthermore, sugar consumption may leave you with a stomach ache, if you each too much of it. This experience of physical discomfort can also trigger or worsen your anxiety. When recovering, it is best to cut out all excess sugar from your diet and focus on healthy fats, vegetables and proteins. Make sure to have protein with every meal.

Alcohol

Alcohol interferes with the brain's communication pathways, and can affect the way the brain functions. These disruptions can change mood and behavior, and make it harder to think clearly and move with coordination.

Alcohol can affect our mood because it can affect the level of serotonin in the brain. Serotonin is a feel-good brain chemical that—when in short supply—can cause feelings of anxiety and depression. Alcohol also affects blood sugar levels and can cause drops in blood sugar. A drop in blood sugar can cause dizziness, confusion, weakness, nervousness, shaking and numbness. The nervous system is also affected by alcohol, particularly during a hangover, because in order for the body to fight off the sedative effects of alcohol, it puts the body into a state of hyperactivity to counteract this effect. This hyperactivity can lead to shaking, light/sound sensitivity, and sleep deprivation. Your heart rate can become elevated as a result of consuming alcohol, which can cause a palpitation false alarm and put you into a state of anxious anticipation. This is why you should stay away from drinking for the time being. Although alcohol can help some people feel less anxious, since it is a sedative, the rebound effects are not worth it. I know that for me, alcohol made my anxiety even worse, and didn't really do anything to calm me down.

RULE 15:
No Processed Foods

I would highly recommend either going on a ketogenic diet or a paleo diet. Ketogenic diets are great for stress and anxiety because they naturally increase GABA levels in the brain. GABA is the primary inhibitory neurotransmitter in the brain, and is responsible for calming us. It is like our natural Xanax. Ketogenic diets also help the body maintain stable blood sugar all day long, since the body switches from using glucose (sugar) as its primary fuel source to ketones (fats). This means fewer highs and lows throughout the day. Ketogenic diets have also been shown to reduce inflammation in the body and help people with IBS. Since anxiety causes a lot of digestive issues, such as IBS, keto really shines in this way. I know that it worked very well for me when I used it. However, sudden dietary changes can also be a stressor to the body, so ease into it over time by gradually reducing your carbohydrate intake until you reach about 30 grams. If this is too strict for you, I would follow a paleo type of diet that stays away from processed foods, which can cause vitamin and mineral imbalances that affect your energy levels and mood. Processed foods also contain many ingredients that lead to higher levels of inflammation in the body, which has been linked to depression and mood disorders. Stay away from most high-sugar fruits, unless they are berries, and keep your carbohydrate sources complex and slow-digesting. You can find a good list of such foods here: https://ultimatepaleoguide.com/paleo-diet-food-list/

These are just general guidelines for anyone who wants to be healthy and live a more optimal lifestyle. These guidelines are a great starting point for anyone who is just getting into healthy living for the first time. However, to get the most out of your nutrition, I recommend a more targeted approach for my clients. With my clients, as a functional medicine practitioner and nutritionist, we typically do a few functional medicine tests that determine the nutritional status of the body, hormone levels, stress levels and potential food and environmental allergens. We use these results to create a nutritional program that will assist in your recovery by focusing on adrenal health, lowering inflammation levels and encouraging hormonal balance. Having high levels of anxiety and stress already causes a depletion of certain nutrients, such as magnesium and B vitamins, so nutrition is an essential aspect when healing from anxiety. Having high levels of sustained anxiety also changes the way we react to certain foods and our ability to remove toxins from the body, in addition to influencing our hormones and inflammation levels. Applying a specifically tailored program can target all of the areas that are lacking, allowing us to sustain the body as it moves towards recovery. The power of nutrition to lower inflammation, balance cortisol levels, and maintain hormonal balance goes a long way in recovery, and afterwards to sustain a long and healthy life. Having lower levels of inflammation has been shown to reduce feelings of depression, fatigue and anxiety. Hormones also play a critical role in the way we feel on a day-to-day basis, so ensuring proper hormonal balance is key in any recovery program. One cannot go without the other. A holistic mind, body and spirit approach must be used when healing the nervous system. Everything is connected, and healing the mind and body should target the person as a whole, not just individual sections.

RULE 16:
Practice Gratitude/Goal Setting

You can't be grateful for what you have and still be anxious. This is why I always tell my clients that practicing gratitude is key. I would highly recommend getting a small journal and when you first wake up in the morning, think of 5 things that you are grateful for that you already have and write them down. I also suggest writing down 5 things you're grateful for that you *don't* have yet, but write them down anyway, as if you already have them. This breaks the habit of waking up in the morning and checking in on how you are feeling. It removes the focus of your thoughts from yourself and negative rumination, and shifts it instead to something positive and uplifting. This is a great technique to use to break this pattern in the morning. This small and simple step will assist in creating new neural pathways in the brain for long-lasting happiness. It also helps the mind create a belief of gratitude through repeated action. Being grateful for something that you want and believing that you already have it creates an energy within you to manifest and draw those things into your life. Gratitude is all about building momentum. It's about starting off your day with a new habit, and breaking old unproductive habits that keep us ruminating on the negative aspects of life. I know that practicing gratitude was a huge part of my recovery, and I'm grateful that I kept these habits in place throughout my recovery. Another additional practice is to write down 3 things that you're going to do for the day and set one small goal that you know you can accomplish. Even if that goal is to go get groceries from the store down the street. Setting these goals and then achieving them gives you a sense of accomplishment and generates good feelings, which is helpful for anyone, not just anxious people! By setting small goals and achieving them every single day, you begin to build confidence and momentum, which opens up more possibilities for you. It makes your world look bigger and bigger, instead of smaller and smaller. Reaching and accomplishing goals results in a sense of fulfillment and pride, even if it means just leaving your house for a short walk. The goal here is to create another new positive habit that will change your life for the better! Finally, at the end of each night, open up your journal and write down what you're grateful for again and what went well that day! Be thankful and mean it! This gives your mind something positive to think about before going to bed. It is a great habit that I still do to this day. Starting and ending your days in a positive way is a great approach to help yourself feel better over time.

8

Recovery Time

- Everyone will recover at their own pace, so there is no set time for recovery. For me, it took about a year to understand and know what TRUE acceptance was. After that, I cured myself using this method within a few months' time. Getting the acceptance piece down is what takes the most effort and time. Once you're there, you will be set free!

Recovery from anxiety is never a linear pathway. It's more of a rollercoaster ride while blind-folded without a seatbelt, but if you follow the rules, you will recover in no time. It has to happen because all habits are learned and all habits can be changed. Think of anxiety like quitting smoking. You must quit behaving, thinking and acting anxious in order to quit being anxious. It's hard and uncomfortable at first, because you're so used to it, but I promise that in time you will see great results. Recovery can feel like climbing a mountain and then falling back down again, but each time it will get a bit easier and you will fall less and less hard until, finally, you return home. Recovery will look a lot like this:

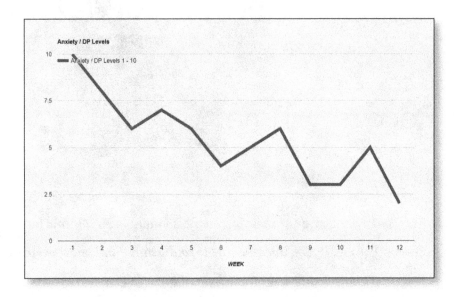

What you must remember is the big picture. Even though one day or week may not have been as good as the previous one, you are generally moving towards a lessening of symptoms. Don't worry about feeling good one day and feeling bad the next; just be there and accept every day as it comes. Don't try to figure out why you felt better yesterday or last week just to find all of your symptoms back in full force today. This is draining and exhausting. Just surrender to it all, accept it all and let the universe do its magic.

-Do NOT put a time limit on your recovery. Again, that's only telling you that there's something in your life that needs to be monitored or cured. Simply follow the guidelines outlined in this book, live your life as normal and watch recovery come to you!

Summary

Well, that's all I have to share. I really hope that you enjoyed this book and can relate to it on some level. I hope that I've inspired you to take charge of your life and live a life of connection, freedom and happiness again. I know you can do it because if I did it, so can you! Keep up the hard work. I am looking forward to hearing from you as you recover from this temporary blip on your lifelong radar!

To sum up:

1. Anxiety is simply a highly sensitized nerve state that is being kept alive by fearing and resisting it.
2. Anxiety is a habit of thought and behavior.
3. Anxiety is a collection of stored memories of past experiences in the body.

4. Anxiety can be fully reversed by the body's own natural processes once we move out of the way.

5. Depersonalization is simply chronic brain fog from consistent inward anxious thinking and checking in.

6. DP/DR is just a trauma coping mechanism that is actually trying to help you and is completely harmless.

7. Remember that with anxiety and depersonalization, you are not actually going crazy, nor are you really sick. These are simply sensations that are re-occurring because of the habits you create.

8. The only way to recover is to move through your thoughts, feelings and sensations.

9. Acceptance, giving up and diversion are the only ways to fully recover in a healthy way.

10

FAQ

-In this is FAQ I use fake names to hide the identity of the people that reached out to me with questions

John asked me:
"How do you control anxiety?"

I replied:
You can't control it, the need for control is what makes you anxious. The key is to not control or cope, it's to recover. Now to assist in this process you can eat healthy take some KSM66, or 5htp but these are coping mechanisms, they are healthy and good for you no questions asked. Having to be in control is a characteristic of anxiety itself. When we try to control ever outcome, and predict what might happen next, we live apprehensively and become impatient. The moment ceases to exist as we habitually try to control the future that doesn't really ever come. It's a never-ending chase, life becomes

a means to an end, like a child on a merry-go-round, going in circles and never getting of the ride. This future oriented focus takes us out of the present moment and into an anxiety state. See where everyone makes the mistake is, that they want to control how they feel. People with anxiety tend to be highly intelligent, perfectionists that don't allow themselves to make a mistake and be human. The pressure of being perfect and holding up your image feeds the cycle of anxiety. The belief that you are in control and need to be in control to be safe from something bad happening is anxiety. It's a future oriented way of life. This means you are not really present but are constantly watching and waiting for what might happen next. In reality what happens next is never in your control anyways and never will be, being in control is an illusion of the ego. To recover and revive a sense of total control is to give up the controlling and trusting that the universe is already doing the work for you. That's where freedom is.

Alex asked me:

"So, we just try to not care about it?" "Try to forget it?"

My reply:

This is a very common question that I get a lot. Trying to not care is a mistake people make as well. By trying to not care or focus on our anxiety is actually putting more effort and focus onto the anxiety itself. It is actually a form of coping, running, and avoiding. The key is to fully be there with it and accept it deeply as a part of what you are experiencing in this moment. Fully allow its presence within you knowing that these feelings are not important. Knowing these feelings are temporary and harmless and that once you finally just let go of trying to do anything about them your body will recover in time.

Trying to stop caring or trying to forget it means you are actively focused and worried about your recovery. All anxiety wants is a chance for you to notice it and allow itself to manifest through you. It's trapped energy, when we avoid, run, distract, "try to forget "or "try to stop focusing" we are actively suppressing this natural happening. This pushing down and pushing away of anxiety fills your body up with more and more of it. If you think of your body as a jar, and the contents of the jar is the anxiety. If you are practicing acceptance then you are allowing the jar to open. As the jar opens just a little you let some of the repressed anxious energy out creating more space within the jar. So, you accept and let go for a while and some of your anxiety leaves the jar. Instead of continuing to open the lid and letting the trapped anxiety out, the next time your anxiety symptoms show up, sometimes with higher intensity, you suppress it, you fear it, you become anxious about it. What this does is it refills the space we just emptied with more anxiety which never allows the jar to empty fully. This is what the anxiety cycle is. With recovery, the empty space begins to grow larger and the anxiety energy begins to grow smaller. That is why it is a gradual process that can feel like a roller coaster ride.

Sometimes we will open the jar and release, and sometimes we will add back into the jar, but all in all that it okay, because eventually the empty space in the jar becomes larger and larger, so even if we add some back in our anxiety symptoms never come back with the same intensity. The goal is to finally empty out that jar and return back to baseline, and it is possible to do over time.

Alice asked me:

"What can I try to make anxiety go away?

I replied:

Anything that takes effort means extra pressure. Anything that involves trying means your attention is on the anxiety and making it go away which is the anxiety disorder itself. It is a paradox. When you actively try to make it go away all of your attention is still given to the anxiety itself. It is a habit of being preoccupied with yourself, your thoughts and feelings. The key is to accept and trust that your body and mind will heal themselves.

Lauren:

"I have accepted my anxiety, and been trying to let it go, but why is it not going away?"

I replied:

Lauren, if you are using acceptance as a coping mechanism to try to get rid of your anxiety, then you are missing the point of acceptance. If you are going about your day judging whether or not you are accepting properly, or having doubts if true acceptance will work then this is actually resistance. True acceptance is something that happens deep down to your core. If you are accepting to make the anxiety go away, then deep down inside something within you is holding onto the idea that it is not okay to feel this way right now, and that you must do something about the feeling. If you are so focused on the acceptance and recovery you are never allowing yourself to focus on your goals and living your life, which are the keys to recovery. You are actually becoming anxious about your own recovery, which in turn continues the anxiety cycle.

Matthew asked me:

"What about lifestyle, caffeine, drugs?"

I replied:

I believe your lifestyle is very important, but it is not the entire picture. Of course, removing anything that would stimulate your already stimulated system would be an intelligent decision. Things like nicotine, caffeine and other uppers would help mitigate some of the symptoms, but usually won't be the cure. Using drugs during your recovery is also harmful and defiantly can make things a lot worse for you during your recovery. Having a coffee here and there will not totally destroy your recovery. Remember that recovery focuses on using the tools I described here in the book!

Ellie asked me:

"Will I ever be my old self again?"

I replied:

Do you really want to be your old self again? It is the old self that brought you to this point of developing an anxiety disorder, and there is nothing wrong with that. This is why having anxiety and depersonalization is a huge blessing. This is because it forces you to make changes in your behaviors and life. You have now been given a blank canvas, a second chance at life! Anxiety and depersonalization have given you the opportunity to create a new identity, one that is strong, beautiful and confident. Creating a new self is not easy, and it will take a lot of trials and errors. While in the process creating your new identity important to learn to set boundaries and create an environment around you that doesn't promote fear and negativity. This is an ongoing learning process throughout your recovery and even beyond it. Learning to say what you mean when you mean it. Learning to say no when you mean it. Putting yourself first before anyone else, and deeply realizing and understanding that this is not selfish. Putting yourself first is an act of self-love, and allows you to recharge so that you can present your best self for others. Self-love allows you to be open to giving more love to those that matter the most to you. Another big one is learning to stop needing the approval of others and to quit people-pleasing all the time. These behaviors just drain all of your energy.

Developing the skill of not caring what others think, and learning to rely on yourself frees up so much pressure from the world. When we realize that we are all that same, and that we are not special we can relax. No one really cares what's happening in you, what you are feeling or thinking about. This is because they are so focused on themselves, their worries and their problems.

Contact Me

During your recovery process, feel free to shoot me an email with any questions. Check out my webpage as well for some free blogs and up-to-date information on health and wellness. If you want private one-on-one coaching, please feel free to shoot me an email. With one-on-one coaching, I assess my clients via phone, Skype or email, and use some functional diagnostic tests to create an integrated approach to recovery. I design specific nutritional plans, workout plans, and lifestyle adjustments, while assisting in creating a vision for your life. I also focus on goal-setting and moving forward with your dreams. Everything I teach my clients, I practice myself. I am a firm believer in creating a full mind and body approach to healing and maintaining wellness. For those that enjoy a group setting, I have also created an 8-week program of recovery that delves into all the steps and helps create a space where people come together and motivate one another to stay accountable when applying the program. In my program, I dive more deeply into the topics that I have discussed in this book. For more information, please contact me!

Jerzy Roginski Jr

jerzyanxietyrecovery@gmail.com

READER NOTES

READER NOTES

READER NOTES

READER NOTES

READER NOTES

CPSIA information can be obtained
at www.ICGtesting.com
Printed in the USA
LVHW020927210221
679521LV00005B/631